HOW TO CATCH TROUT!

By Lee Straight

ILLUSTRATIONS BY NELSON DEWEY

BC Outdoors

"Saltaire Series"

Published by **Special Interest Publications**
 Division of Maclean Hunter Ltd.,
#202-1132 Hamilton Street,
Vancouver, B.C. V6B 2S2

First Printing: March, 1973
Second Printing: March, 1974
Third Printing: March, 1975
Fourth Printing: May, 1976
Fifth Printing: November, 1977
Sixth Printing: February, 1980
Seventh Printing: May, 1984

Printed in Canada by Universal Printers Ltd.

Canadian Cataloguing in Publication Data
Straight, Lee, 1915-
How to catch trout

Oringially published: Sidney, B.C.:Saltaire Pub., 1973
ISBN 0-88896-145-6

1. Trout fishing.   I. Title.
SH687.S87 1984   799.1'755   C84-091327-3

ABOUT THE AUTHOR

Lee Straight has a long and varied experience in many aspects of outdoor living and recreation. He was fish-and-game editor for the Vancouver Sun for 33 years and travelled widely, pursuing his many outdoor activities.

He has fished in the first world series of fishing in Florida and has angled for big game fish in Hawaii, Florida, the Bahamas, Mexico, Northwest United States, Alaska, Europe, New Zealand and Tasmania. He is the holder of several big fish trophy buttons including a 65½-pound diamond button tyee salmon (taken unguided at Comox), a 135-pound Pacific sailfish, a 35-pound Pacific dolphin fish and a 40-pound Atlantic kingfish.

At home in British Columbia, Lee's first love is salmon and trout on light tackle, though his occupation dictated his keeping in touch with all methods. He has taken a 10¼-pound rainbow trout on cast fly from shore, as well as many steelhead, coho salmon, and even pink chum salmon on cast fly and all other recognized sporting methods.

He is married with two daughters and a son, all married.

INTRODUCTION

INTRODUCTION

The man who keeps his line in the water longer has a better chance of catching trout, and it helps if he has the right lures or baits.

Even more important, he needs to be where he can show his lures to fish. Putting it another way, he needs to be where the fish are! But **where** to fish is not the subject of this book. Rather, we offer basic methods and even "tricks," if you like, on how to catch freshwater fish, mostly trout.

I wrote this with a string (old piece of fishline) on my finger to remind me that this manual is aimed at the beginner. It goes without saying that any manual is, as they usually say in publicity books, "also useful for the expert."

Several sages, in essays on angling, have told of the progression of the angler through the main steps in angling sophistication. Roughly, they are:

1. To catch a fish.
2. To catch one often.
3. To catch many.
4. To catch a large fish.
5. To catch fish in a difficult manner; that is, on tackle that is ultra-light or that requires greater dexterity.

I guess I'm hovering between the fourth and fifth stages but, through my job as a newspaper outdoors writer for almost 30 years, have had to keep in touch with anglers in **all** stages. Most are fine chaps. Their sportsmanship is unrelated to their skill or progress. The few that I despair over are those who become skilled, remain at the second and third stages and release only a few captures, just so they can display their catch (prowess) to friends, wife or kids.

I hope this little volume will quickly assist anglers past the stages of just catching a fish and that they will, just as quickly, give serious consideration to progressing into stage five. We anglers are multiplying much faster than the trout. We just cannot keep hauling in "limit" creels, once we've proved we know how.

Keep your back-cast out of the bushes.

SPECIES OF TROUT

RAINBOW

According to some taxonomists (the chaps who decide how to name animals) only one true trout originally occurred on the North American continent, aside from the Atlantic salmon. That is the **rainbow**, from which the **steelhead** or **sea-run** variety, the several **mountain** and even **grand cutthroat** are claimed to be offshoots.

The North American fishes, particularly those of the northwest, still are evolving after the last ice age of only 20,000 years ago. It is likely the cutthroat would have become a definite species, rather than the controversial species it's become, if man hadn't interfered.

Generally, the true trouts carry the generic name **salmo**, and include only the **Atlantic salmon**, the **rainbow** of North America and the **brown** (or

German) of Europe. The rainbow's generic name is **Salmo gairdneri**, after a scientist named Gairdner. The various offshoots considered to be subspecies carry a further name, such as **Salmo gairdneri gairdneri** for the **steelhead**; the name gairdneri being repeated to denote what is considered by the majority of taxonimists to be the original species. It sounds right. The **steelhead** is a sea-run **rainbow** and all life started in the sea.

Most call the **cutthroat, Salmo clarki,** after another scientist, but a very few suggest it be called **Salmo gairdneri clarki.**

I CHRISTEN YOU...
SALMO... GAIRDNERI... FRED

CHAR

There are other "trouts" in the salmonoid family which are typed as chars. These include the **lake char** (or trout) that occurs all across North America's north, the **Dolly Varden char** of the Pacific coast, the **Arctic char** of the Arctic slope and even the eastern **brook char (speckled "trout"** or **brookie**), occurring naturally on the Atlantic slope but introduced in the west as a good winter fish because it is more active in low temperatures than is the **rainbow** trout.

Y-YOU'D WANT TO STAY ACTIVE... IF YOU LIVED IN THIS KIND OF CLIMATE...

FLAP!   FLAP! FLAP!

The chars, to complete the record, bear the Latin generic name **Salvelinus**; our Pacific salmons, the name **Oncorhynchus**.

GRAYLING, WHITEFISH AND KOKANEE

Also considered salmonoids and caught incidental to other fishing (or deliberately) are the **Arctic grayling** and the **mountain whitefish** (often miscalled **grayling**). Other than pointing out that both are caught in rivers (among trout in the case of the whitefish) and that the grayling usually have Arctic watershed rivers to themsleves in B.C., we'll not dwell upon those somewhat "coarser" fish except to admit that they are edible and much better than no fish at all.

We mustn't conclude without recognizing the **kokanee**, a resident and usually, but not always, landlocked race of sockeye salmon. The **kokanee** (**redfish, kickininnie**) provides an interesting and often prolific fishery, is very tasty and takes trolled bright lures best, though it can be taken on cast fly or spoon.

DISTINGUISHING CHARACTERISTICS

All salmonoids have the tiny, fleshy fin on the back of the "wrist" of the tail, just in front of the tail or caudal fin, called the adipose fin.

Whitefish and grayling are the least trout-like, having large scales--fewer than 100 along the lateral line (halfway up the side). The grayling has a very large dorsal fin, with more than 20 rays (rib-bones). The whitefish dorsal is smaller than a grayling's but larger than a trout's, having fewer than 20 rays.

If the fish has normal size scales, more than 100 along the lateral line, it is a trout, char or salmon. If the anal fin, underneath the center of the body, behind the anus and in front of the tail, has 12 or fewer rays, it is a trout or char; if 13 or more, a salmon.

Since this book is concerned with trout, we won't delve into the distinctions among the Pacific salmons. (See "How to Catch Salmon," by Charles White, Saltaire Publishing, Sidney, B.C., $1.50)

If the fish has teeth on the shaft of the vomer, which is the small bone in the roof of the mouth, just back of the nose, then it is one of the trouts. The distinctions among the trouts are less definite. Generally, the rainbow's mouth outline does not extend back of the eye, it has no teeth on the back of the tongue, where the gill-rakers form a "V", and has no red slash in the fold under the lower jaw.

CUTTHROAT

Generally, the cutthroat has a larger mouth, extending past the back of the eye, has those hyoid teeth on the back of the "tongue", and has the red slash. But the sea-run varieties of cutthroat sometimes are so silvery that many of their markings are obscured. Sometimes their growth is swifter and their condition higher, so they have smaller "button" heads, with daintier mouths, that do not extend back of the eye. Males have larger mouths than females.

All in all, it's an indefinite process of distinguishing cutthroat from rainbow, served better by familiarity. I find myself relying on spots and color--the yellowish cast and larger spots usually showing on the cutt.

The brown trout, introduced into a few waters in B.C. has still darker and larger spots, many surrounded by halos, and is generally a darker, brownish fish, hence the name.

CUTTHROAT

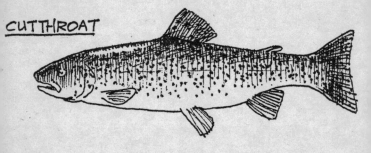

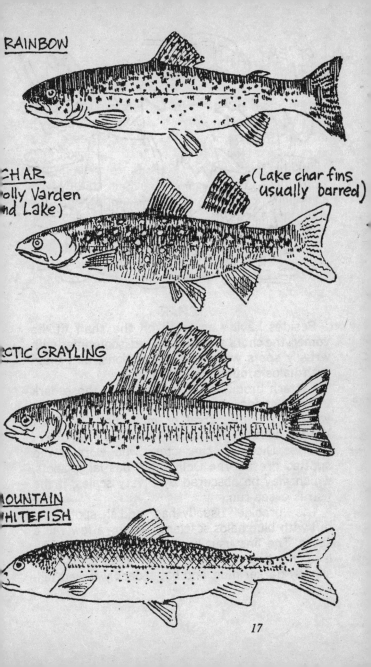

RAINBOW

CHAR
(Dolly Varden
and Lake)

(Lake char fins usually barred)

ARCTIC GRAYLING

MOUNTAIN WHITEFISH

CHAR

Besides having no teeth on the shaft of the vomer, the chars are well spotted, sometimes with wriggly spots we call vermiculations, and often with halos around some spots.

Eastern brook and lake char have those dark vermiculations on their back and almost invariably on the dorsal or main fin. The Dolly Varden doesn't. The "Dolly" is named after one of Charles Dickens' characters who wore a red spotted dress. The Dolly often has large spots, which may be obscured by silvery scales, if the fish is a sea-run.

The "brookie" usually has reddish spots, too, but with blue halos scattered among a few white spots. The fins usually are edged in white. The lake char has only light, almost white spots on a slightly darker hide, and has a deeply forked tail.

TROUT SIZES

Lake char and steelhead trout are the largest of the trouts, the lakers run to the 30-pound mark in the N.W. and double that, east and north. The record is a 102-pounder that had been naturally caponized or castrated, caught commercially in the far north. The rod and reel record is 65 pounds, from the Northwest Territories. Forty pounds is tops in the northwest. A 39-pounder was caught in Okanagan Lake, B.C., where char aren't supposed to occur, in 1970.

ABOUT TROUT

RECORD CATCHES

The steelhead sport record is a 42-2, troll-caught in Alaska, and 43 commercially in B.C. It is a 36 on the rod and reel from the Kispiox River, B.C. Usually they run around 10 pounds.

Resident rainbows commonly surpass 20 pounds in large lakes and usually occur at under five pounds in smaller lakes, can be mature at less than a pound. They reach greater size in lakes than in rivers.

Cutthroats can reach good size in lakes and occasionally in the sea, up to 12 pounds in a few lakes. More often they're a half-pound for the maidens, up to two or three pounds for the mature fish, either at sea or running into rivers to spawn. The colorful mountain variety of cutthroat is almost always less than a pound, however plump and frisky it might be. Some sea-runs around five are reported annually. The world record is an incredible 41 pounds from Nevada; not impossible, as many heavyweights come from there.

Eastern brook char reach the five-to-10-pound size in interior lakes where they've been stocked, but usually are closer to a pound, roughly parallelling the Kamloops for size when sharing the same waters.

Dolly Varden commonly run to 10 pounds, with a B.C. record of 40 pounds from west Kootenay's South Slocan River.

Grayling are usually about a pound, reaching nearly six pounds.

Mountain whitefish are about the same but I've yet to catch or see one over two pounds.

Kokanee salmon usually are well under a pound at maturity but in rich waters commonly reach two or three pounds. The odd kokanee attains the growth of the sea-run sockeye on occasion, reaching the record size of nine pounds, either by being a glutton or having a malfunctioning pituitary gland.

The true trout generally spawn in late winter, through spring, invariably in running water. The chars and kokanee spawn in fall, and white fish spawn in late fall to mid-winter. Grayling spawn in spring.

TROUT FOODS

All the trouts, chars, whitefish and grayling, seek roughly the same food: from nearly microscopic plankton up through fly larvae, fresh and saltwater shrimp, ghost shrimp, copepods ("lice"), worms, leeches, terrestrial flies and even their own roe (eggs) or their own or other varieties of young fish. In other words, **anything** may be snapped up by these fish.

They even swallow bits of wood, pebbles or feathers. Much of their "biting" is thought to be in anger or in defense of self or mate from any threatening or merely passing object. That's why these fish are game fish; game for anything, at times.

DISTRIBUTION

Rainbow and cutthroat trout originally occurred commonly on the Pacific slope of North America, from Alaska to Mexico; rarely in the adjacent waters of the Arctic watershed; and scattered in the odd mountain lake of the Rocky mountain range.

They since have been introduced successfully, and are usually outstanding game fish, in Chile and Argentina and other parts of South America, in Eastern North American waters, Europe, Asia, Africa, Australia and New Zealand—Not everywhere in the world, but world-wide distribution.

Dolly Varden char had about the same original distribution but were easily fished out. They rarely remain common except in wilder waters, thankfully including B.C.!

Lake char are in almost any large lake and many associated streams east of the coast range.

Mountain whitefish distribution isn't entirely mapped but it seems to be anywhere in the province. The lake whitefish occurs only in a few lakes of the northwest.

Grayling occur on the Arctic slope of B.C. The

"...AND IF YOU LIVED IN WATER THIS COLD -- YOU'D BE A LITTLE GRAY AROUND THE GILLS TOO!

FLAP FLAP

Montana variety is to a limited degree found in the southeast corner of B.C., in Idaho and Montana.

Brown trout have been successfully established in a few lakes and rivers of the northwest.

Eastern Brook trout have been introduced in many lakes of the interior, particularly the south Cariboo and the southern Kootenay of B.C. and many lakes in the northwest U.S.

QUALITY

The trouts and Dolly Varden char are almost indistinguishable as to quality of flesh, species-to-species. There is a greater variation in the individual's condition. A fat, non-spawner rainbow trout is much tastier than one in spawning condition. That difference may be somewhat less obvious in spawning kokanee salmon; still less obvious among the chars; and hardly noticeable in whitefish and grayling.

The change in flavor is a matter of reducing fat content of the flesh. Spawners feed little, gradually consuming stores of fat, and gradually tasting "drier". Or, as I like to put it, more and more like the so-called coarse fish, which are bland and "blooey" of flavor.

SEA-RUN ARE TASTIER

Generally fish are tastier if sea-run. Partly because they are more distant from spawning, therefore in better condition, and partly because they seem to dine on better-flavored fare. Also, if they eat crustaceans (either asea or in fresh water) their flesh quality gradually takes on the red "carotin" shade of shrimps and smaller crustacea.

In Argentina, for example, the trout dine copiously on a very red, small crab which turns the trout flesh almost blood red. No appreciable effect on the flavor, other than general tastiness, but so-o lovely and red.

The flesh of lake char on the other hand, can be greasy and moist with fat, yet lacking flavor. As one fishing friend put it, "They taste more like a rockfish than a rockfish does!" Given a choice, I'd prefer the rockfish (a sea fish called rock "cod") unless the lake char is smoked - truly delectable!

Mountain whitefish is less tasty than the commercially fished lake whitefish. I find it a bit rubbery and, again, bland. But it is pale pinky-white and flaky and enjoyed by many.

Grayling is great! Delicate, white, juicy and not bland. It is about the only fish among all those discussed in this book that **needs** to be filleted from the bone and skin though we all like **any** fish filleted (from the bone but not the skin). for a change.

LIFE CYCLES

All true trouts, including the Atlantic salmon, are capable of spawning a second or third time,

(some even a **fourth**) but few of them make it. Some rivers have a large proportion of steelhead that spawn a second time. Most do not. But there isn't the spectacular general die-off after a spawning, inevitably faced by the five Pacific salmons. Sighting of a dead, spawned-out trout is rare.

Most spawn in their third year but they break every rule. Some rainbow trout spawn when they're four or even five, or maybe never. Some develop spawn and don't deposit it, resorbing it into the system if they can't reach what they consider suitable spawning conditions--usually a good flow of clean water over clean gravel.

As with the salmon, the young live a while in the

running waters where they're hatched, then move upstream or down into still waters to grow, just as the salmon migrates to sea. Like the salmon, they return to the river of their birth to spawn. Time

spent at their birthplace varies from only a few days, a year or two, even to permanent residence. Then there are trout populations dwelling entirely in rivers. Spawning on beaches, with mild success by some Pacific salmon, is not common with trout. And as far as I can find it has never been successful.

Dolly Varden and eastern brook char spawn in running water but lake char can spawn on reefs in lakes. Chars reach greater ages than the five to eight years of the true trouts, with some lake char attaining 30 years or more.

There is little reference in literature to the ages of mountain whitefish or of grayling, but they seldom die upon spawning. Since most fish continue to grow until death, it's safe to say these species likely live only five to 10 years.

READ THE REGULATIONS

Readers no doubt have heard the old saw about the independent bloke who had trouble assembling a Christmas toy, only to have his missus tell him, "If all else fails read the directions." That applies to anglers, too. The folder containing **fishery regulations** usually is issued with the renewed licence. No matter how well you **think** you know them, read them again! Maybe not much literary charm there, but several annual changes and it's full of reminders.

If you're trying new waters, look them up in those regs! There may be something unusual to watch for--upper reaches closures on streams, short closed seasons to protect spawning runs and so on.

READ THE
REGULATIONS!

TROLLING

PRINCESS ITALIA

RODS

Trolling for trout from a boat can be done with any rod and reel but you can get by nicely with sea-angling tackle. The difference is the terminal gear. But, for lake trolling only, the best rod is light, one as long as you can tolerate. Most trolling rods tend to be too short. Two long rods, nine-foot or longer, spread the lines so well that a third even may be used off the stern of the boat with less chance of tangling. A heavy fly or steelhead rod is good for lake surface trolling but a typical sea rod is better for trolling a long, deep wire line.

REELS

Any reel will serve, so long as it will hold 100 yards or more of 15-pound line for general trolling, but for deep-trolling a sea-reel with 100 yards of monel wire and another 100 of backing is preferred. Some winter anglers on the large lakes surface-troll with 100 or more yards of line lying like gossamer behind the boat. There, too, you'd need 200 yards.

SINGLE ACTION

Single action reels are more fun with which to play fish. The typical fly reel qualifies except that it has no hub-nut to tighten and hold the line from being stripped out by a long, heavy troll. Popular sea reels of the single-action type, with such a hub-nut, are best for big lake trolling.

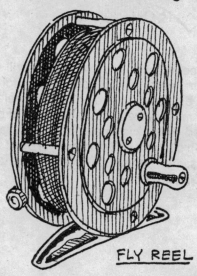

FLY REEL

A "single-action" reel is one with no gears -- one turn of the knob or knobs causes one turn of the drum. They come "caged" as with flyreels, or uncaged, as in the case of many sea-reels favored in B.C. Another name for an uncaged, single-action reel is "center-pin" as the axle pin is the total support of the reel drum.

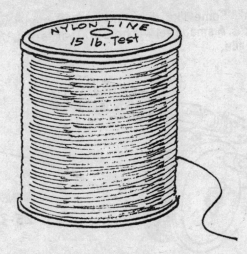

LINE

Any line is suitable for general lake trolling but monofil (single strand) plastic line (nylon or dacron) is favored because of its durability, good handling characteristics, freedom from birds-nesting, relative translucence in water, and low cost. Ten-pound-test is strong enough for all B.C. lake fishing but rather filmy for handling. I prefer 18-20-pound-test, stiff or hard monofil for lake trolling.

The man who mainly likes to cast, or who wishes occasionally to try, can get by nicely by trolling with a fly rod, reel and line, or a spinning outfit. Spinning (fixed spool) reels are balky for playing a fish but many use them for trolling.

For deep trolling with monel wire, the .028-inch gauge is handy, the same that is used for sea-trolling by those who can tolerate its tendency to kink. Some like the thinner .018 monel wire in lakes. A small reel will hold 200 yards of it, but it is fragile.

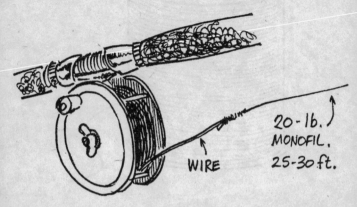

WIRE

20-lb.
MONOFIL.
25-30 ft.

The end of the wire should be twisted neatly into a tiny loop, then about 25 feet of 20-pound-test monofilament line tied to it. That keeps the wire neatly stowed on the reel when not in use, and is better for attaching sinkers and lures.

The sinker should always be fastened a rod-length above the lure; a **slip**-sinker much higher as it can be removed or slipped down as the fish comes to the landing net. I'm surprised at how many interior anglers fasten their lure right to the end of a sinker, then the sinker to the line. They do catch fish that way in virgin water, but would do better to move sinkers up the line.

LURES

There are literally thousands of good lures for trolling for trout, which fall into a few classes, allowing the northwest angler to keep his tackle box relatively uncluttered.

LAKE TROLLING

Most successful but least fun, often hooking fish and drowning them undetected by the angler in the boat, is the lake troll. It is sometimes called **Jack Lloyd, gang troll** or **pop** gear, and has a rudder blade followed by one to six large spinning blades of brass, nickel, chrome-plate, enamelled

LEADER

BLADES

RUDDER

Plastic beads on wire hold blades in place, allow them to rotate.

or hammered metal. Behind it is trailed a small plug, winged drifter or fly, or a hook baited with real or artificial garden worm, insect larva, cluster of fish roe, a few single fish eggs, a bit of canned shrimp, kernels of corn or even bits of marshmallow.

WORMS

Worms never have lost their place as the preferred bait for trout. In trolling for kokanee salmon, a winged-bobber (or "drifter") is effective. Some use a small fishing plug behind lake trolls.

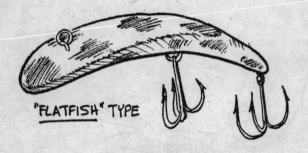

"FLATFISH" TYPE

VIBRATION PLUG

That brings us to the **next** to most effective, but far more sporting troll, the trolled vibration plug, usually shaped with a shovel-nose that makes it jiggle rapidly. One brand has outsold all others combined but several shapes and sizes are effective. All brands and shapes come in many colours, more popular of which are the fluorescent red, silver, red-spotted-white, green frog and yellow-spotted black.

SPOON

Another good lure, an all-round item, since it casts well in lake or stream and also doubles as a steelhead or salmon spinning lure, is the striped, wobbling spoon. Usually nickel, copper or brass material, it is unpainted on the concave surface, painted white with a red stripe on the convex surface, often in a hammered finish, with fluorescent red edges. Copper usually produces best for me.

So equip your tackle box with a lake troll (unless the sight of one gives you the same rash it gives me), a few two-inch vibration plugs and a few striped, red-white casting and trolling spoons.

Best hook size for bait is No. 4 or 6. Sinkers may be needed on the line, particularly in summer, when fish are deeper. A few slip-sinkers, one-to-four ounces apiece, are handy.

TROLLING METHODS

For purely trolling, one should have rod-supports, particularly if alone in the boat. Most trout are taken on a line trailed only 20 to 35 yards back of the boat, without weight, but I like a single, small (half-ounce) sinker to quickly submerge my terminal gear, particularly with wooden plugs. If trolling close to lake shores, which usually is the best water, be cautious about using weight. It can snag you in weeds and sub-merged logs.

British Columbia laws permit trolling two rod-reel set-ups if the angler is alone in the boat, but

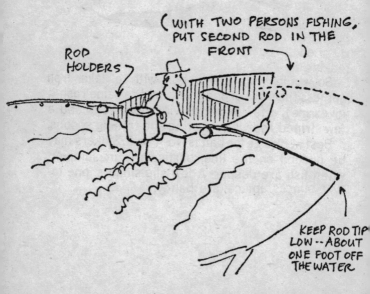

(WITH TWO PERSONS FISHING, PUT SECOND ROD IN THE FRONT →)

ROD HOLDERS →

KEEP ROD TIP LOW -- ABOUT ONE FOOT OFF THE WATER

the practice isn't easy, particularly with weighted terminal gear, sinking flyline or wire line. It is even worse in the shallows. That's when it helps to use floating trout plugs that come to the surface when you slow down to handle one rod or to play a fish. Floating lures also help when putting out two lines, the first floating out of harm's way until the second can be paid out. This is particularly ticklish if the angler has no motor.

If the surface or sub-surface trolling fails to produce, try a two-ounce sinker. Lake trolls will sink about as deep without a sinker as will a plug with two ounces, at the same speeds.

Though spoons are of metal, they sink little deeper than wooden or plastic plugs. A few plugs are made to dive. Watch them; they really do. They can be used without added sinker.

All plugs are designed to dive but the floating plug trolled from an unweighted line must be watched to see that it dives cleanly when you resume forward motion. The hook can catch on the leader or line, snagging it so it doesn't submerge, or it may spin, twisting the line and seeming to discourage, rather than attract interest from fish. Some plugs spin or pop right out of the water if trolled too swiftly.

TRY CLOSE TO SHORE

Another alternative in trolling is to shorten-up line and travel tight against the bank of the lake, maybe only an oar's length out. Still another -- troll a very, VERY long line, 100 yards - or even twice that. But you need plenty of room on a large lake, or a small one almost to yourself. Winter trollers on Okanagan, Shuswap and Kootenay lakes troll that way -- really quite exciting, with no weight, just a plug or spoon and a cranky, muscular trout of one to 20 pounds tail-walking 'way out back of the boat.

TROLLING SPEED

Most freshwater trolling is done at a dead-slow speed but exceptions can be made with large plugs or large spoons in lake trolling. In other words, troll faster when imitating minnows or other forage fish. The "gang" lake trolls have so

many blades whirling they're almost impossible to troll fast. Like the vibration plug, the lake troll is a "busy" lure that needs little forward speed for good action.

Trolled flies will be discussed under flyfishing.

STILL FISHING

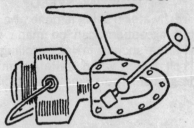

EQUIPMENT

Most popular still-fishing rod-and-reel is the casting outfit, usually a fixed-spool, spinning reel. A line can be let down into a lake or paid out into a stream from any reel, but casting it saves much time and, in the case of the stream, the bait or lure can be placed further from the bank.

Spinning reels cause beginners to lose many fish and even the skilled angler can lose the odd one. The slip-drag is just too jerky to coax or yield to fish the way you can with an easy-running, revolving-drum reel. But spinning reels **are** so simple to cast and are easily the most popular. Most anglers reason, rightly, I suppose, that first they have to hook a fish, **THEN** worry about landing it!

Line-test-strength also is non-critical - five to 15-pounds is fine. A good outfit for river or lake, would be a steelhead rod and revolving drum reel. The long (over nine-foot) steelhead rod allows the bait-plunker to cast a bobber-float, plastic bubble or quill float with greater spacing between bobber and bait. A flexible-tipped rod is pleasant as it reacts better to the fish's runs and, in fact, is more relentless than a stiff rod-tip as it prevents the fish from getting slack line.

BAITS

Best baits for streams are: real or synthetic earth worms, maggots, larvae of flies (often called "hellgrammites" after the larva of one such fly, the **dobson** fly), single and cluster fish roe, grasshoppers, crickets, canned shrimp, live or cooked ghost shrimp, bits of fish flesh.

The same baits are effective in lakes, with the addition of dyed bits of sponge, colored cocktail marshmallows, kernel corn and plastic copies of fly larvae.

Live minnows or any live fish except **game** fish are prohibited as bait in B.C. and parts of the northwest U.S. That is to discourage importation of such coarse fish and thereby accidentally colonizing lakes with them. The various shiners and minnows, once established in a lake, can compete with or replace game fish.

In streams the baited hook or slowly "working" lure is hung off the main line on a six-to-12-inch dropper. The main line is held in place with a sinker at the end of the line.

HOOKS

Only one hook is permitted on a line in B.C.,

except in the case of bar-fishermen on tidal waters of the Fraser River below Hope; with fly-casters who may augment the usual end or anchor fly with one or two droppers. A technical exception is allowed under the regulation stipulating gear designed to catch more than one fish at a time. "Stewart Tackle", for example, is an assembly of three single hooks or two singles and a tiny treble, tied in tandem, each thrust into a garden worm, but the entire package designed to catch only a single fish.

I used to like Stewart hookups but a still-fishing specialist convinced me that I could do as well with a single hook in a worm, allowing the trout time to gulp the entire worm, then hooking it as effectively.

He said he found more of them do so if fewer hooks bristle from the bait.

Many fast-water trouters believe the same, preferring to donate a few worm-tails, plucked off by trout, just to keep them coming and eager for the next bait hook floated over them. Multiple hooks versus single hooks always have been a moot point among anglers.

STILL-FISHING METHODS

Fishing in quiet river pools, or in lakes, one need just chuck out his bait and sinker and let it lie. But that leaves much to chance. Many--I among them -- prefer to dangle all baits from a float. The clear - plastic bubble float has the edge, but any cork, balsa or hollow plastic bobber also is effective. Most action is just off-bottom, but if the water is deep, as in a lake, you can thread your mainline through a float with only a tiny hole, slightly bigger than the line. Then tie a simple overhand or figure-of-eight knot in the line as a stop. The

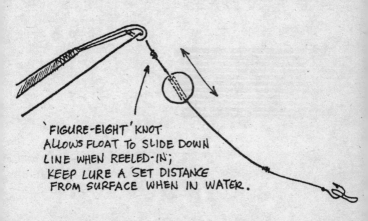

`FIGURE-EIGHT` KNOT
ALLOWS FLOAT TO SLIDE DOWN
LINE WHEN REELED-IN;
KEEP LURE A SET DISTANCE
FROM SURFACE WHEN IN WATER.

knotted line flows easily through the rod guides and onto the reel, allowing you to reel in until the float slides up against the leader-top or sinker or whatever the rig. Then, upon being cast, the lure snakes out to the target area, sinking and drawing the line through the bobber until it stops at that cunningly located knot, suspending the bait clear of the pool bed or lake floor!

This works with all baits, but in the case of artificial worms, it is often better to retrieve very slowly or let one's boat drift, rather than working a still bait from anchor. In streams, I like the artificial worm at the end of the line, below a shotted leader, as in steelhead fishing, rather than dangling that phony worm from an anchored leader, too obviously inert to take a fish.

LAKE FISHING

Still-fishing is very productive in lakes. Selfishly, I suppose, because I don't enjoy such sedentary fishing, I wish it **weren't** so productive! Skilled still-fishing will take more and larger trout than will any other method. I like to work at my angling, feeling less like a meat-angler that way. Forgive me if I'm unimpressed by the sight of a couple of quiet killers, at anchor nearby, cranking in two fish for my one, some of theirs huge by the standards for that water.

I'M GONNA MAKE YOU AN OFFER YOU CAN'T REFUSE!

With cutthroat trout, particularly in wild, lightly fished waters, strips, or even chunks, of fish flesh, sometimes from another cutthroat, are effective. "Wild" cutthroats appear greedier (more resourceful?) than do Dolly Vardens, which are noted for their gullibility. Cutts aren't above gulping fish strips right where you might also take them readily on the fly.

The strip of such fish should be small or your quarry may rob the hook without feeling its point. Either a small strip off the belly of another trout, little more than a bit of skin, or a small cube of fish flesh with some skin attached, will take cutthroats. As with most still-fishing for trout, such baits seem to select larger fish.

When cutting strips of fish as bait for trout, they usually produce better if kept tiny, little more

than skin. Note that, at the time of writing this, strips of fish of any kind as bait were legal only on Vancouver Island, the mainland coast and northern regions. **Not in the Kamloops, Cariboo, Okanagan or Kootenay regions!**

In stream fishing, artificial salmon eggs or worms are effective but are a poor substitute for the real thing if used in still waters. Anglers can preserve their own single salmon eggs from "ripe" skeins taken from gravid steelhead, coho or chinook salmon by separating the eggs in a saline solution of water (add salt gradually until the solution will float a potato).

The eggs are bottled with just enough of the brine to keep them immersed. Cochineal or other vegetable dyes can be added, mostly to please the angler. I've never seen proof that pale, preserved eggs are less productive than when tinted.

These single eggs are fragile and suitable only for stillwater angling. River-trouters need a tougher egg. I recommend the commercially prepared, bottled single salmon eggs sold in most sport shops in various shades of pink or red, even in cheese flavor.

If the angler wishes to try preparing his own singles for river fishing, I recommend one of the commercial recipes, described so well in How to

Catch Steelhead! by Alec Merriman.

Alec separates the eggs from the roe sacs with warm water but I prefer the salted water mentioned above. But I like the toughening formula. Here is Alec's "witch's brew":

"Six cups of eggs, two tablespoons of borax (not the type with a soap additive), two tablespoons of table salt, two tablespoons of benzoate of soda, and the dye (or cochineal).

"The mixture is added to six cups of cold water, brought to a slow boil, stirred and eggs tested every half-minute for firmness. Fish-hook penetration is used to test the eggs. The outer skin should be tough, the interior soft.

"Once the eggs are firm, they are dumped into a bathtub or other container of cold water. The eggs then are drained and packed, right to the brim, in eight-ounce jars containing an ounce apiece of glycerin, sealed tightly and inverted a few times to coat the entire surface of each egg."

Clusters of roe are preserved best by cutting them into bait-size chunks, laying them on some layers of newsprint to drain momentarily, dredging them in fine borax powder (not with added detergents), then bottling or storing in plastic cartons, and deep-frozen until needed. They keep for days at normal temperatures in the borax powder but gradually become yellow, hard and less productive.

FISH CANNIBALISM

Once trout attain a fair size, to continue growing they must drift into cannibalism, and certainly become otherwise carnivorous in order to maintain that extra bulk. That's the principal reason still-fishing, with sizeable, meaty baits, attracts larger trout. The big trophy fish waste less time searching for tiny fly larvae and indulge ever less often in snacks of hatched flies, hence are rare catches on dry fly tackle.

ICE FISHING

Another form of still-fishing is that done through holes in lake ice. Some anglers, and I'm one, frown on ice-fishing, not only because of its sedentary nature, but because they feel lakes get enough of a cropping by the more traditional fishing methods in spring, summer and fall. Also, it makes me feel like Nanook of the North waiting to shoot a seal in the ice-hole!

Some lakes, however, support good stocks of the introduced eastern brook trout, which in winter bite more freely than do rainbows. Such lakes deserve some exploitation through the ice. Wisely or not, ice fishing was made legal on our trout lakes some 20 years ago, merely by lifting the winter closure. Until it's made illegal, many enjoy it.

A hole is cut in the ice, usually over not-too-deep water and usually near the lake edge. Lines are suspended either to the lake-bed, out of sight of the angler, or with the lure or bait hung in sight so that the angler can jig, swing or spin, or otherwise agitate the bait or lure.

BAITS

Baits favored are: kernel corn, bits of canned shrimp or fresh meat, worms, fish eggs, roe, or any land or water insect larva, either the grubs from rotten stumps or the caddis cases and "hellgrammites" raked from the mud under the ice at the lake edge, or from a stream.

It is illegal to remove freshwater shrimps or other crustacea, which would include the tiny mysis "shrimp."

With small trout, small baits are better, otherwise the fish pick the baits off the hooks, bit by bit, rather than gulping the parcel. Some ice-fishermen like a generous worm but must tend it, ready to jerk it as the fish nibbles, just as must the perch fisherman in tidal water.

LURES

Lures are often effective for ice-fishing, particularly for kokanee salmon. Spoons with red, beady "eyes" or fluorescent red edges seem best, always agitated or jigged. It's rare to take trout with a dangling, stationary lure and not common to take kokanee that way.

BRRRR!

LINES

Line strength for ice-fishing is incidental except where trout, either rainbow or lake char, run to great size -- over three pounds, say. Then one needs 15-pound-test or stronger. The strength of one's leader, as always, is a matter of balance between the need for subterfuge and that for strength. With the leader hanging motionless, there is no doubt the fish is aware of it. One should keep it as thin as he dares, while retaining a chance of landing that fish without breaking the leader. I like 15-pound-test for jigged lures, as the moving lure takes attention away from the leader. With baited hooks, short, thin leaders of as little as five-pound-test are usually adequate if the line is 15-pound or heavier. The line endures any rubbing against the ice-edge until the fish is tired.

USE GAFF HOOK

Landing nets are of course useless for this game, but a stiff-handled, sharp-pointed gaff hook is handy. That is unless it is known that all the fish, whether trout or kokanee, will be small -- under two pounds, say. If over two, or if char (which run to great size) are possible, then a gaffhook is a **must!**

The fish is played to a standstill, which usually doesn't take too long in that frigid water. Then it is gaffed by running the gaffhook down into the hole, parallel to the line, giving a quick lift of the gaffhook into the side of the head area, then slithering the trophy out of the hole.

That, to me, is the most exciting part of ice-fishing -- sometimes the **only** exciting part! Make sure that the gaffhook point is so keen it hurts your eye to look at it.

ICE FISHING METHODS

Holes are easily drilled in the ice with ice augers, preferable to chopping or power-sawing, as they are much smaller and less hazardous when abandoned. All abandoned holes should be marked so that skaters and subsequent anglers won't stumble into them in the dark or after a snowfall. Only one line is allowed per ice-fisherman, as with all still-fishing. That line must be tended: not necessarily held onto, but watched.

At the time of this printing, two lines per ice angler were legal on lakes in angling region 7, the northern region. Region 7 is fish and wildlife management areas 20 to 28. However, it would be advisable to check with the fish and game regulations before setting out.

It is illegal to spear, snag or club game fish in British Columbia. But so-called coarse fish, including ling, a freshwater cod, (but not char) may be speared if trapped under the edge-ice of a lake, e.g. the much storied, but seldom practical herding of fish by skating them when seen through clear ice on Lac La Hache.

ILLEGAL TACTICS

It is also illegal to use snares, lights or firearms for fishing, or to leave fish offal or other deleterious material, which means litter, on the lake ice when fishing.

Also illegal is another form of littering, of inestimable damage to lake beds. That is the practice when ice-fishing of scattering fish eggs, corn, meat, bones or eggshells, either to attract fish, as with other illegal ground-baiting, or to make a light background against which to see fish hovering near one's lure or baited hook. Conservation officers are particularly watchful for this.

Any rod-reel-line combination can be used for ice-fishing but many specialists like a very short rod or even just a stick, with a reel and one or two line-guides mounted upon it. Some use "tip-ups", which involve a teetering device that triggers a flag-waving arm or mounts a reel so that its ratchet can be easily heard from nearby. It is illegal to leave set lines, but one is considered to be tending his line if nearby, chatting with other anglers, or huddled against the cold.

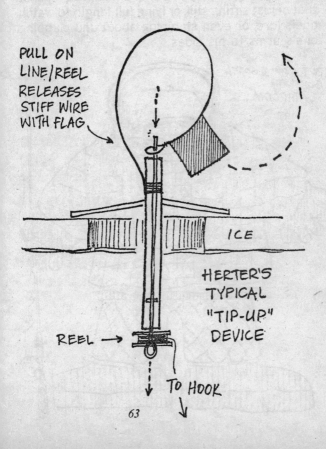

PULL ON
LINE/REEL
RELEASES
STIFF WIRE
WITH FLAG

ICE

HERTER'S
TYPICAL
"TIP-UP"
DEVICE

REEL →

TO HOOK

KEEP WARM!

Types of preferred clothing and shelter seem endless. Some use war surplus flight clothing, snowmobile suits, flight boots or greatly oversize rubbers or mukluks, padded with sox. The neophyte ice-fisher usually thinks he's going to freeze to death. It is difficult to appreciate the difference in blood circulation resulting from some bracing hockey or social skating, as against that of just sitting still, or lying full-length to watch one's lure, or even stamping about and clapping one's arms to his sides.

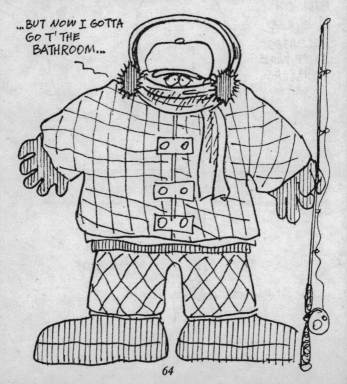

...BUT NOW I GOTTA GO T' THE BATHROOM...

WHERE TO "GO"

The matter of toilet facilities is in fact, the greatest single problem, other than catching fish, that faces the ice-fisherman! He must tote his own toilet, go into nearby woods or sneak a go right on the lake ice when no one is looking -- an inexcusable ploy in this day of large population and rampant pollution. Think about all that when you plan to swoop down on some likely lake!

SHELTER

Completely wind-proof outer layers of clothing are a must. Many anglers erect a plywood "V" of two slabs, or a crude shack. The sophisticated ice-fishing houses of the east are well publicized.

The northeastern North American angler in general is so deprived of readily accessible game fishing that he has made quite a thing of ice-fishing. One writer described a classy ice-fishing shack as a small golf and country clubhouse on runners, with a hole in the floor (to fish through, of course). Many include the sort of chemical toilet used in motorized campers.

CASTING

Most popular casting outfit for lake or stream is the spinning reel and matching rod of various sizes to match the job in hand, but still so versatile that it will serve for all trout fishing, lake or stream, large fish or small.

REELS

The term "spinning" in this country has gradually followed the United States terminology, which specifically means fishing with a fixed-spool reel (called the "threadline" in the United Kingdom). The British angler uses, and the western Canadian angler **formerly** used "spin-

CARE TO GO FOR A SPIN, OLD CHAP?

ning" to describe the art of casting with any whirling or wobbling lure, from any reel. It includes the center-pin, revolving drum reels, usually used for so-called "coarse" or "rough" fishing in public waters; the caged, single-action spinning reel used for salmon, pike and some sea-fishing; the level-wind, revolving drum reel also used for salmon and pike; and finally the fixed-spool reel.

SPINNING REEL

In the United States and eastern Canada and ever more commonly in B.C., the terminology goes as follows:

A spinning reel has a fixed spool, usually with a bail, occasionally with just a finger, which bail or finger revolves around the spool, winding the line upon it. To cast, the bail is swung aside, cocked out of position while the cast is made. Winding the handle first flips the bail back to gather line, then starts that bail revolving. To play a running fish, the otherwise fixed spool can revolve, with an adjustable drag as the line is tugged, but doesn't revolve when line is being gathered.

This reel, because it doesn't over-revolve when casting, is less inclined to permit loose, sloppy coils that might tangle or "birds-nest". So it is the easiest to master for casting. Conversely, it is the fussiest for carefully playing a fish, once hooked, and is conducive to the greatest percentage of fish lost through either panic treatment or slow reaction to the movements of the fish. The spinning reel is found in all grades and prices, from a couple of dollars to almost $100. The

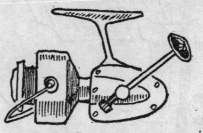

quality is in the positive, gradual adjustment of the drag and the durability of small springs and wearing surfaces.

One further advantage of the spinning reel is - that it will cast very light lures further than will other reels.

Greatest disadvantage, other than difficulty in playing fish, is that the spinning reel has the most moving parts and breaks down most often. This reel usually is mounted below the rod, well up the handle from the butt.

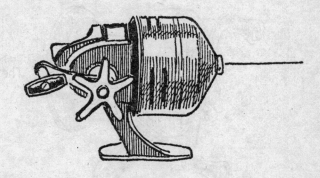

"SPIN CASTING"

Growing more popular, particularly where fish are small and reel-capacity need not be great, is the "spin-casting" reel, which combines features of the spinning reel with those of the plug or bait-casting reel, next to be discussed. Simply, the spin-caster encloses the line-winding action in a conical cover, has a fixed-spool with slip-clutch and usually is mounted atop the rod handle, with a thumb-tip push button to capture the line for casting, rather than using one's finger tip.

Disadvantage of this reel is limited capacity, resulting from need for more cumbersome mechanism and housing. First models were poor but many now are reliable items. I dislike this model because so much of the action is hidden under the cone and line seems more liable to jam, and so more difficult to free-up tangles. Just not a reel for British Columbia.

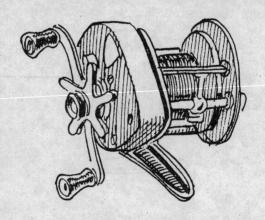

BAIT CASTING

Probably the most common style of reel for casting in North America is the **plug - or bait-casting** job that mounts atop the rod, handy to the thumb for either single-or-double handed casters. The handle revolves on the original models but more recent versions have, like some sea-reels, a free-spool disconnector, leaving the handles at rest when the spool whirls during a cast, but allowing the handles to take over for the retrieve. A further refinement for freshwater casting, also borrowed from usually larger sea-models, is the star-drag type of slip-clutch. It may be confusing to a person at first, but it doesn't allow a fish to crack one's knuckles during a battle!

The models of bait-casting reel normally sold are rather limited for the large trout and waters encountered in B.C. angling, carrying around 100 yards of line, or less, adequate only for eastern bass, pike and other coarse fishing. We like 200 yards out here for larger trout or long-line trolling, or for reaching out on large rivers, when casting with the same outfit.

More recently, European models (copied by a few U.S. and Japanese firms) have developed better carrying capacity, retain the handy and

neat level-wind principle of storing the line evenly on the spool, have on-off click ratchet, a free-spool lever and a star drag. The plug-casting reel is the most accurate for casting to a target and more suitable than the spinning or spin-casting reel for playing fish, particularly if it is the older model without the star-drag. It still is not so "sweet" for playing fish, however, as is the old fashioned, British single-action reel or the fly reel.

RODS

Once the reel is chosen, one should seek reliable advice about matching it to a rod, with appropriate reel seat and rod-guides. Most people use rather short rods because they are cheaper and seem handier. Often, neither the salesman nor the shopping angler know their sport and may have been exposed to too much misleading eastern angling literature, illustrated with those short boat-and-plug casting rods that may be adequate only for small fish or in confined situations.

HOW MANY FEET, SIR?

If the reader already owns a short rod, not to worry. It's merely a fine point and not critical. Those equipping for the first time will do better for a combined lake- trolling- casting rod if it is no less than eight feet long, preferably nine, even ten. The usual types of rod used by the B.C. steelheaders or by salt water salmon anglers for stripcasting or mooching are perfectly suitable for lake-casting. They're suitable for **all** casting except, possibly, along tiny streams -- or when you're **ONLY** casting from boats on lakes, where great distance isn't a problem. There, you simply can row closer and make your cast!

So, for lake casting, only, **I'd** be happy with an eight-foot, medium stiff casting rod, with a "fast" or whippy tip if it is to wear a spinning, spin-casting, or plug-casting reel. I'd want a slower but thicker tip, limber all the way down into the handle, if it's to be used with a single-action reel or a free-spool, plug-casting reel.

LINE, LEADERS

I'd store no less than 200 yards of 10-to-15-pound flexible monofilament on any reel except the large, single-action type. In that case I'd prefer the rather more durable, less kinky hard or stiff nylon, in the same 10-15 pound breaking strain.

In lakes, you need use no leader with fairly heavy lures like spoons and metal plugs. In their case, 10-pound-test line allows somewhat freer casting, using the line itself as leader, right to the lure.

Leaders aren't needed merely to save line. That idea is a hang-over from the days when we considered fishline expensive, and when test-strengths were so unreliable we didn't know where a line would snap when we leaned into a snagged lure or a heavy fish. Nowadays, you can point your rod straight down the line, being careful not to rub a week spot in it against the sides of the tip-top guide ring. You lean back and carefully pop free the line when a lure is snagged. It almost invariably snaps at the line-to-lure knot, giving your line back. Chances are that any line not snapping there has a weak spot. If broken somewhere back of the lure, it likely was ready to discard anyhow.

CASTING METHODS

When casting for fish, success usually favors the deeper retrieve. You cast, allow the lure or bait to settle, then slowly retrieve, sometimes varying the speed just for variety to perhaps provoke a strike from the fish. In lakes, that is safe enough, unless you are so foolhardy as to let the

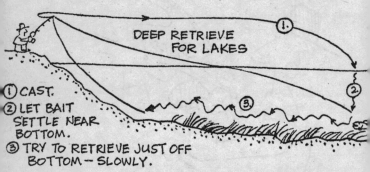

DEEP RETRIEVE FOR LAKES

① CAST.
② LET BAIT SETTLE NEAR BOTTOM.
③ TRY TO RETRIEVE JUST OFF BOTTOM -- SLOWLY.

lure settle right onto a weedy or snag-studded bottom. In running water, you must learn to gauge the depth so as not to lose lure after lure to a rocky bottom. Or you can cast with a bobber that holds the lure or bait generally short of the riverbed or just discreetly wiping it as it drifts down-current. With an artificial lure, cast generally straight across current, let the lure settle a moment or two, then start to retrieve, endeavouring to skim the lure close to the bottom. The retrieve usually must be speeded at first,

RUNNING WATER RETRIEVE

① CAST.
② LET BAIT SETTLE TOWARDS BOTTOM.
③ RETRIEVE QUICKLY AT FIRST; SLOWER IN MID-CURREN QUICKLY AGAIN IN SHALLOWS.
④ OR... USE BOBBER TO KEEP BAIT JUST OFF BOTTOM.

gradually slowed as the lure swings down-river from the cast, retrieved very slowly up the bank, then swiftly again as it nears the rod-tip and the extreme shallows.

The knack is soon acquired. Its mastery is one of the great attractions of river spin-fishing (casting) with or without a bobber!

Many river anglers use leaders to separate added sinkers from the lure or bait, a handy device as one learns to feel the sinker knock bottom, or the rock-tops. They then speed the retrieve before the lure can jam into trouble among the stones or in a snag or strong weeds. For river trout, usually much smaller than steelhead, I use any light casting rod and reel, preferring any small revolving drum models of British or Canadian style. My lure is hung on the end of a two- or three-foot, five- or ten-pound test leader, joined to the main line by a small (No. 6 or 8) barrel swivel. Sometimes I dangle a two-to six-inch length (depending on the speed of the current) of three-sixteenth or one-quarter-inch lead wire from a thinner piece of line a couple of inches long, secured also to the top ring of the same swivel.

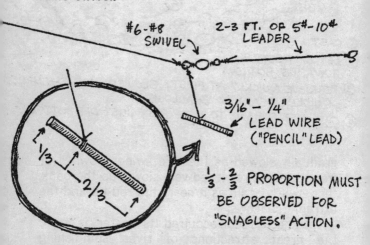

#6-#8 SWIVEL

2-3 FT. OF 5#-10# LEADER

3/16" – 1/4" LEAD WIRE ("PENCIL" LEAD)

1/3 – 2/3 PROPORTION MUST BE OBSERVED FOR "SNAGLESS" ACTION.

1/3

2/3

When I use such a thread to suspend the sinker, I tie it one third the distance from one end of the sinker-wire. It then dangles at about 60 degrees to the leader and often, when it jams between stones, "walks" out of trouble, end over end, when I give it a good tug. If I'm in a hurry, with less time to tie a sinker that way, I snip off a one or two inch piece of surgical tubing, slip it onto the line above the leader swivel, then work the piece of lead wire sinker into the tubing so it is pinched

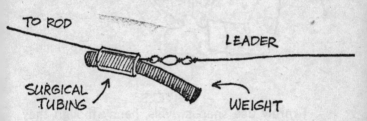

TO ROD

LEADER

SURGICAL TUBING

WEIGHT

against the line by the tubing. Very popular are three-way swivels, with the section of surgical tubing whipped to the dangling third of the swivel, into which the end of a lead sinker-wire can be forced. The latter rigs appear neat and efficient, which they are, but are also troublesome or expensive. I don't bother with them.

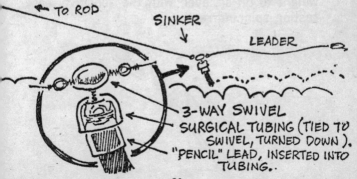

← TO ROD

SINKER

LEADER

3-WAY SWIVEL
SURGICAL TUBING (TIED TO SWIVEL, TURNED DOWN).
"PENCIL" LEAD, INSERTED INTO TUBING.

SWIVELS

I rarely use snap swivels, handy though they seem, ready on the end of a prepared leader. It makes just that much more expensive and obtrusive hardware at the head of lure or bait and is very little speedier than the improved jam knot. Some lures are sold without swivels at the top; **then** a snap swivel is handy. I try to remember to install ordinary swivels on such lures, employing a split ring to do so.

One can cast a small plug but it requires added weight to do so, even with the sensitive, easy-casting spinning reel.

STANDBY OUTFIT

Though I've long stuck with fly tackle for lake and resident river trout, I usually carry a small spinning rod somewhere if I'm heading into unknown territory -- mostly to sample water another way if it won't yield fish to my flycasting. By the same token, the casual angler or wilderness tourist might need such a standby spinning outfit. There are several good models of spinning rod that break down to two-foot or shorter lengths, some encased with a reel and lures, all handy for travel.

LURES

The basic lures for such a kit are the small (1¼- to 3-inch) "S"-shaped wobbling spoon of any finish; or the narrow shouldered, broad-based,

red-and-white enamelled wobbling spoon, copper or brass; some red-white striped, some just "raw" metal. These are most reliable. Add to them: a few flyrod-size "vibration" or shovel-nosed trout plugs; some leader material, No. 4 or 6 nickeled bait hooks or some tied-up or snelled hooks; a jar of single salmon eggs; some whisps of white synthetic wool to drape around the bait egg or eggs with a simple overhand knot; some tiny, winged sinkers or heavy split shot (size SSG or "cannonball"); and a couple of two-ounce sinkers for deep trolling.

You might need a couple of those plastic one-to one-and-a-half-inch bubbles with the tiny plugs,

so that some water can be added for casting distance. Useful while still-fishing a lake or stream, or even to cast a wet fly some distance. Just two flies are prescribed for such a travel kit: a **Tom Thumb**, No. 8 dry, or a **Doc Spratley** No. 6 (wet).

The **Tom Thumb** approximates emerging sedge flies or almost any fully hatched and floating fly. The **Doc Spratley** looks like any number of sub-surface lake or stream creatures. The Tom Thumb should be allowed to rest five or ten seconds then jerked slightly. That simulates an insect trying to decide whether to fly away, rest awhile, lay an egg or expire, a sight often witnessed by a prowling trout.

The Spratley should be very slowly retrieved -- just one speed faster than dead stopped. Most aquatic life has negligible forward locomotion. More about that under flycasting.

Remember the cardinal rules about casting in rivers! -- If you aren't knocking bottom with any lure but a dry fly, you're usually just not fishing! And if you don't lose the odd lure then you aren't knocking bottom! In lakes, try many depths but, except with flies, rarely retrieve near the surface.

FLY FISHING

Fly casting is really no mystery. You can speedily learn to get by with a flyrod well enough to catch trout. But fly **FISHING** still is the most intricate, richest and least generally mastered kind of angling! You may soon learn to cast but the **use** of that casting knowledge and all that goes with it is a lifetime study. That's why many fly fishermen seem overly proud of their interest, but don't mistake them. If they do seem to feel superior to the non-flyfisher, it is as justified as the pride of the champion golfer over the weekend duffer. Give the fly fisherman his due. He sets a high mark and tries to reach it.

There is one major exception. That's the angler who quickly appreciates that in his fishery, mostly lakes, say, the fly more often than not is the greatest producer. Then it becomes easier to demonstrate one's prowess, with fish in the creel. I point this out by way of showing that fly fishing is not necessarily a self-denial except, perhaps, in winter steelhead trout fly fishing, fly casting the sea for salmon, or other "far out" sophistications.

Fly fishing has many advantages. Its lures, the most expendable part of that fishing, are the cheapest, smallest and easiest to make or carry,

aside from bait. Once a rod, reel and a line or two are procured, additional equipment need not be fancy, expensive or extensive. There is expensive fly tackle, just as there is expensive spinning or trolling tackle, but it isn't required so much as it is pleasant to use and a pride to own.

RODS

Flyrods, even before the days of synthetics, came in low-cost materials such as second-grade, split-and-bound, Tonkin cane; greenheart or lancewood. Cheap cane now has become rare but plastic rods are such good substitutes while still low-priced, that only experts or specialists appreciate the difference between cane and plastic (resin-bonded fibreglas). And some even prefer the ultra-lightness of the "glass" tube over the more solid-reacting but heavier split-cane rod.

About half the cost of a good rod, irrespective of the basic rod material, lies in the fittings and the quality of their assembly. All good rods will outwear several sets of the world's finest line-guides if heavily used. Each new set requires complete stripping down of the rod finish and careful rewinding.

Few anglers, however, fish often enough to quickly saw their line through the rod rings (or guides), so this feature isn't appreciated by many. I never hesitate to advise the casual or beginning fly-rodder to buy a cheap but not junky glass fly rod. If he takes to the sport, fishing often, he'll move into better tackle and make his own decisions about specially hardened rod rings and quality reel seats.

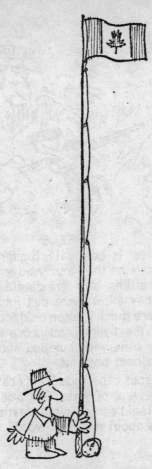

SIZES

A good all-round rod-size for B.C. flyfishing is eight, eight-and-a-half- or nine feet in length. We need the rod mostly to cast the line and, since most of our B.C. flyfishing is on brawly rivers and breezy lakes, that calls for distance work. A nine-footer isn't too long, despite what eastern, small-stream, dry-fly-tossers write and claim.

REELS

Any fly reel is adequate, though I dislike the cheap models as they loudly advertise their low price by rattling and grinding like bent egg-beaters. They allow more dirt into their works, corrode more quickly, often hold too little reserve line under the flyline, and prove less rugged if dropped or otherwise bumped about on stream rocks or in boat bottoms.

I prefer split cane rods for fly casting but own and use several of glass. For trolling and spin-fishing, as I said earlier, glass-plastic is so durable that it has about replaced wood.

LINE

The most important part of the fly fishing trio of rod, reel and line is the line. Fly lines actually are slim, sleek, plastic-coated, braided ropes, usually of nylon in the floating variety, or of dacron in the sinking variety. Nylon itself is lighter than water, dacron just heavier.

Recent exceptions are made of homogenous plastic, drawn and shaped through dies, somewhat transluscent but otherwise like braided, coated fly lines. The solid plastic line also is weaker than braided lines but stronger than the leaders used between line and fly. One of my friends snapped two plastic lines while stretching the kinks out of them.

BASIC SHAPES

There are three basic shapes of line and seven basic weights -- not just total weight to match the strength of the rod, but weight compared with water, which dictates floating or sinking qualities of the line.

In shapes, there first is the **non-tapering** or level line. The **double tapering** line has a long, fat belly section that tapers to a finer point at each end and is reversible. And the line that has a short, fat section just back of the thin tip, tapering down to a thin running line, is called a **forward** or **torpedo-taper** line. In using it, however, you really are casting a length of line like a heavy spinner. The weight of the forward, fat line draws the rest of the line through the guides.

LINE SHAPES *

NON-TAPERING

DOUBLE-TAPERING

FORWARD TAPERING
("TORPEDO")

TO ROD

92

TO LURE/BAIT

* EXAGGERATED HERE

I won't attempt to give casting instructions in this modest book, but the prospective fly angler must appreciate that a fly rod and line are not always used like a long, slim bull-whip. The line is cast so that it is checked by the non-rod or **line-hand** until the moment of the cast, then released to let that forward line draw more running line through the guides. Thus the term, "shooting" line. There are many fine books and pamphlets on flycasting, and in most large centers, several free summer afternoon-evening fly casting schools, conducted by fish and game clubs.

LEVEL LINE IS ADEQUATE

The level line is cheaper than tapered lines, casts well enough and is not nearly such a handicap as many anglers believe. Most hear what a tackle salesman has to say, then settle for a

...IF YOU WANT MY OPINION...

$10.95

$37.50

double taper. That is okay as the level and double-tapered lines can be reversed when they become rough. But torpedo-head lines are non-reversible, expensive and only a slight advantage on lakes. Torpedo-heads are at their best on rivers or for distance-casting on windy lakes, but the difference isn't marked. The beginner can start with level lines and spend his money on extra flies and other tackle.

Level lines of good quality are around the ten dollar mark, often less. Double-taper of medium quality are more expensive but good quality, double, and forward-taper lines, are nearer the $20 mark.

Most useful line for lake fishing is a full floater. Most useful for rivers is a medium-fast sinker. For swift rivers, or for lake-bottom fishing, a fast sinker or high density ("Hi-D") line is preferred.

LINE DENSITY

The seven basic types of line density are the **floater, sink-tip, wet-head, slow-sinker, medium-sinker, fast-sinker** (or **Hi-Density**) and the **lead-core.** A few are custom made or home-made, splicing sections of line for certain work on waters of known speeds of flow.

With the **floater,** only the added leader and wet fly is lying in, or below, the surface of the water. With the dry or floating fly, a floating line always is used.

The **sink-tip** is a floating line with the front ten feet heavier than water, and therefore sinking, for use with wet flies.

The **wet-head** is a sinking torpedo-head of 20 to 30 feet, attached to a floating running line, used also in river wet-fly fishing and always in the weight-forward contour.

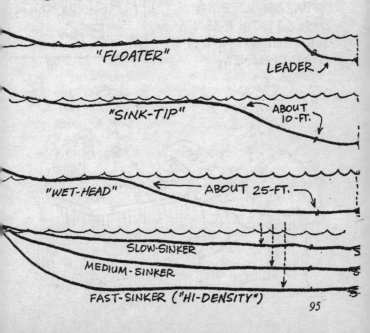

"FLOATER"

LEADER

"SINK-TIP" ABOUT 10-FT.

"WET-HEAD" ABOUT 25-FT.

SLOW-SINKER

MEDIUM-SINKER

FAST-SINKER ("HI-DENSITY")

The three speeds of **full sinker,** plus the **lead-core,** are variously used in rivers and lakes, their speed of sinking matched to the job in hand. Sophisticated lake anglers usually have a **floater, wet-tip, slow-sinker** and **fast-sinker.** Some add the **medium sinker,** for use over certain shoals they find can be fished better with such a medium line.

Sophisticated river anglers like medium and fast sinkers, with a general shift to wet-head versions of them rather than full lines of sinking material. The wet-heads usually are home-made or custom made at a tackle shop, by splicing lines of various materials.

SIX FEET OF SLOW-SINKER... 27 INCHES OF BARBED WIRE...A YARD OF SATIN RIBBON... TEN FEET OF ⅞-INCH POLYPROPYLENE...

HARDWARE, ETC.

HISTORY OF FLY LINES

Before this all sounds too mysterious, let me explain how these lines developed. Their forerunner was the braided **silk** line, coated with specially rubbed and cured layers of linseed oil. Later, the **nylon** line, still coated with oil, appeared.

The silk line had to be further greased with a brand of material known usually as **mucilin,** but other greases or fats were used. A properly greased silk line would float for a few hours then start to sink. As it sank faster and faster, on successive casts, usually from the tip end, the artificial fly lure on the end of the leader became more or less effective. It became apparent that the swimming characteristics of that artificial fly changed enough to make it more or less like the attitude and movements of the freshwater shrimp, leech, snail, minnow or insect larva it imitated.

The real problem was for the dry-fly angler who wished his line to continue to float. The coated, braided nylon line was an attempt to out-float the silk line. It did so, but still sank eventually until substitute plastic coatings which, themselves, are lighter than water, were developed.

That plastic coating started a revolution in fishing efficiency. It wasn't long before an American firm developed a plastic coating that was not only more durable than is rubbed oil but which was heavier, and helped the line sink. Before that development, anglers who wanted a sinking line used a worn silk line that sank better, the older it became; but at best it rated only as a slow-sinker by modern plastic-coated standards.

Anglers wasted much time, after each cast, waiting for line, leader and lure to sink to the depth at which they were encountering fish. Hence, successively faster-sinking line

developments were a boon. All sorts of other improvements resulted or were imagined. At times the fellow with the fast-sinking line, dragging the fly gradually deeper at a 30-degree angle, say, seemed to outfish another angler-line combination. Other times it would be the fellow with the floating line and sink-tip, whose fly drifted along with its nose up, rather than level, or down. From this anglers postulated that the real food must be doing that. They began to study fly larva "attitudes," as well as shapes, colors and speeds of travel (or speed of retrieve of the artificial copy).

To summarize, a good rod for the beginner is an eight-six or nine-foot glass model with a middle-quality large fly reel and a top quality, level floating line. Next step in his development is a second rod and reel, carrying a medium-sinker or a sink-tip line.

LINE WEIGHT

That brings us to the final important technicality -- the total weight of the fly line, irrespective of its floating characteristics, and matched to the strength of the rod. These total weights are designated by the **weight in grains** of the front 30 feet of the line. The sizes run from No. 4 to No. 12. The average nine-foot rod takes a No. 8. That rating applies to all styles of line, whether sinker, floater, lead-core or whatever.

LEADERS

Final part of the fly casting "weapon" is the leader or "trace" which, for all-round lake work,

should be a nine-foot length, tapered down to a 2X or five-pound-test tippet. For tiny dry flies, one must go to 4X or three-pound-test to let the fly float delicately. For lakes with heavy trout or for river work, one needs at least an OX or eight-pound tippet. Droppers or side-tippets shouldn't be added to the leader by beginners, for second and even third flies. They make casting difficult for the beginner and are not a great advantage to the angler.

FLYFISHING LURES

Now for the ammunition. A tremendous selection of lures can be carried in two small boxes, one for dry flies, one for wets.

Thousands of patterns, or recipes, of wet or dry flies exist but exact patterns seldom are critical, except for the expert, who entices those few extra trout that such flies seem to get when waters are stingy. I am going to suggest just a few **dries** that will imitate stone flies, sedges, may flies and gnats when in their mature stage, resting on the water. And a few **wets** that imitate the underwater larvae of those flies, as well as the larvae of the larger dragon-flies and damsel-flies and freshwater shrimp, leeches, snails, water-boatmen and tiny fish fry.

Lake Dry Flies

Tom Thumb No. 10 (the larger the number, the smaller the fly), **Professor** No. 14, **Alder** No. 12, **Black Gnat** No. 12, **Hendrickson** No. 10, any so-called **Sedge** pattern in No. 10, any so-called **Bi-visible** No. 12, any **MayFly** No. 12 or 14.

"TOM THUMB"

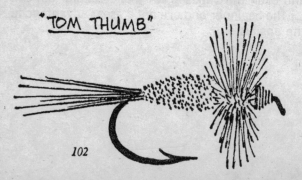

Stream Dry Flies

Any No. 10 or 12 silk-bodied **Bucktail, Tom Thumb** No. 10 or No. 12, **Goofus** No. 12 or 14, brown (and white) **Bivisible** No. 12, Pink Lady **Bivisible** No. 12, **dry McGinty** No. 12, any **Gray Hackle** dry No. 12 or 14, **Tup's Indispensible** No. 12 or 14, **Royal Coachman** No. 14, any **Wulff** pattern No. 12.

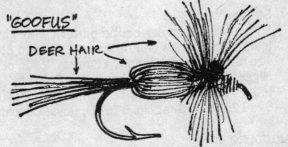

"GOOFUS"

DEER HAIR

Lake Wet Flies

(Unless otherwise stated in Nos. 6 to 10). **Black O'Lindsay, Invicta, Werner's Shrimp, Halfback, Quarterback, Doc Spratley, Green Sedge, Brown Sedge, PKCK** (No. 14 or smaller), **Black Midge Nymph** (16 to 20), **Frank Jansen's Green Sedge, Jack Shaw's Water Boatman,** all **Nation's** patterns but with much throat hackle and wing stripped out (or dressed sparse); any plain chenille-

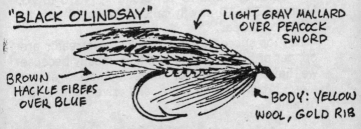

"BLACK O'LINDSAY"

LIGHT GRAY MALLARD OVER PEACOCK SWORD

BROWN HACKLE FIBERS OVER BLUE

BODY: YELLOW WOOL, GOLD RIB

bodied fly, no matter what color; any large pattern (No. 2 to 8 extra-long shank) called "**Leech**," any type of **Muddler**, No. 4 to 10.

Also any fly called a **nymph**, any fly called a **pupa**, particularly any version of the **midge pupa**, usually most effective in simple black silk body, white or light head, no wing, fine chin-hackle.

Stream Wet Flies

Any tinsel or mylar-bodied pattern with wing of teal, mallard, polar hair or bucktail, No. 4 to 8; any size of **Muddler Minnow, Lioness** No. 8 or 10, **Higgs' Gray Nymph** No. 4 or 6, any **Cahill** fly No. 8 to 14, **Professor** No. 6 to 12, **Parmachene Belle** No. 6 to 12, **Black Gnat** No. 6 to 10, **Royal Coachman;**

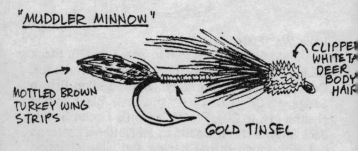

"MUDDLER MINNOW"

CLIPPED WHITE TA DEER BODY HAIR

MOTTLED BROWN TURKEY WING STRIPS

GOLD TINSEL

Polar Coachman or **Polar Royal** No. 6 to 12, **March Brown, Tup's** No. 8 to 14, **Yellow Peril** No. 8 or 10, **Doc Spratley** No. 6 to 10, **Stone fly** No. 6 to 10, **Umpqua** 6 to 10, any fly called a "**nymph**", any fly called a "**pupa.**"

Not too successful in B.C. lakes or streams are popper or balsa or bass-bug flies, mostly because we have few bass; or large minnow-streamer flies, except for trolling and river steelhead fishing.

LAKE FLYFISHING

Most of the food species imitated by wet flies have negligible locomotion, hence retrieving movements of the wet fly should be done **slowly!** Dead-still is fine, except that the fly might eventually dangle vertically or at a great angle from the leader and floating line down into the "weeds." So you must retrieve **verrry** slowly, an inch per second, or in delicate sweeps of maybe six inches of line, resting two seconds, sweeping again, and so on.

When trout are actively feeding, they may seem suicidal and chase a fly larva imitation, even if

stripped through the water 10 times as fast as the top speed of the real thing. But that is push-over fishing, when almost any fly, cast any way, retrieved any speed, seems to work.

When the lake is quiet, the odd fish rising, boiling or bulging -- all different words for a fish that is feeding on surface or sub-surface food -- then an angler must **work** to fool such fish. Casts prove more productive if long and clean, the wet fly settling far from the boat, allowed to rest till the ripples dissipate, then slowly retrieved. If fishing a wet fly into deep water from the shallows over a drop-off, for instance, one usually does best with a slow-sinker. Some anglers specialize in letting their line settle right to bottom, painstakingly retrieving it through the lake floor growth, and catching a surprising number of usually larger fish!

Trout may work right into the shallows, among the roots of the cattail and other reeds, so the angler anchors an easy cast from the lake-edge, uses a floating or sink-tip line and casts into those rises. He doesn't wait too long but still retrieves slowly.

SLOW RETRIEVE IS BEST

Rarely, in my more recent B.C. fishing, have I found that the speedy retrieve, gathering loops of line into the palm, has outfished dead-slow retrieves. I still try because, as a youth, fishing so many "virgin" waters, that retrieve gave me success. Our trout are pounded hard and are wiser now. I have one interior friend who never, just never, retrieves swiftly, despite the success such speed might give someone near him. Usually his patience pays off, proving the quickly retrieved fly success was just luck.

Few are the flyfishermen who never troll their fly. Most so-called flycasters troll much, even **most** of the time. They may be unskilled in casting or in finding likely locations, or they may be just too impatient to make long casts from an anchored boat, so are content to sit there, spending several minutes trolling each cast. Too, they often find more success when drifting before the wind, with the line streaming out behind the boat. An angler can even get in a wink or two of sleep doing that!

I think by now I've made the point -- that **wet fly** success is usually greatest with a very **slowly** moving fly.

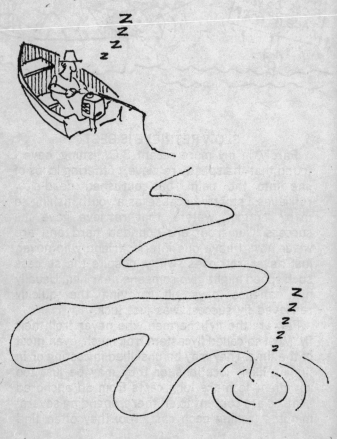

DRY FLY TECHNIQUE

Dry fly technique is different. The angler casts out his fly, preferably up-wind, if any wind is blowing. He lets it float, gathering any slack the

wind puts in the line, so he can quickly lift his rod and drive home the point of the fishhook when a trout runs its lip over the fly.

He can vary his presentation. He can make his cast, gather most of the slack, not disturbing the fly, just watching and waiting for the take. Or he can gather all the slack, give the fly a twitch, wait half a minute, gathering further slack, give another twitch, and so on.

STREAM WET FLY

On streams, the wet fly is usually cast across-current. Fish usually hook themselves against the pressure of the flow on the line-belly. If the line or fly repeatedly snags bottom, one must cast more directly down-current. If the fly isn't swimming deeply enough, cast up-current.

SMALL STREAM CASTS

Small streams often put the angler right across the flow from likely lies for trout. When cast, the line bellies so badly with the midstream pressure that the fly swims down-current too directly. This can be corrected somewhat by "mending" line soon after the start of the drift. With a floating line, or a wet-head line with floating running line, one can mend line any time during the drift.

The term "mending", in casting, alludes to the practice of rolling or flipping the middle part of the line upstream if the middle current is carrying that mid-section downstream so much faster than the leader and fly that the fly skids in or over the current, or darts too quickly downstream.

The mend delays that swifter pressure on the line.

Hence, with dry fly stream fishing, always done with a floating line, one can prolong the drift of the fly without the skidding that usually alarms trout.

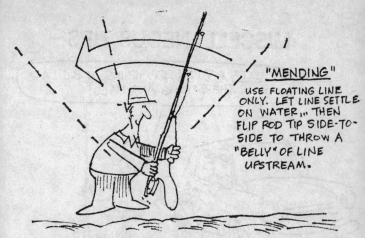

"MENDING"

USE FLOATING LINE ONLY. LET LINE SETTLE ON WATER,," THEN FLIP ROD TIP SIDE-TO-SIDE TO THROW A "BELLY" OF LINE UPSTREAM.

Usual routine with the dry fly is to cast well up current, gathering slack as the fly floats down, guarding against that tell-tale skid.

There are times when advanced anglers deliberately skid or skitter a dry fly, even casting downstream to a trout, just for a surprise tactic, or to imitate a "travelling" sedge or other fly, laying its eggs in the stream, or some land insect merely in trouble with the water.

By "skid", we anglers mean the unnatural movement across-current, either by just travelling faster than the flow or holding back against the flow. "Skittering" is a bouncing, jerky movement, as against a steady skid.

And there are times that the wet fly can be fished from a floating line by casting upstream and quickly retrieving slack, giving the sub-surface wet fly the look of a dead-drifting nymph.

MISCELLANEOUS TIPS

Best fishing season in B.C. lakes is spring and fall, particularly for flyfishing but generally for trolling and still-fishing.

In the warm summer waters, trollers can fish below the too-warm surface layer with less trouble than can fly fishermen. The spinning or vibrating lures used by trollers seem to bring more response from fish made otherwise indolent by those generally warmer waters.

In British Columbia streams, the best fishing is after the peak level of spring-summer freshet caused by the melting snows. With smaller streams, made "dirty" or nearly opaque by glacial silt or just plain mud, the post-freshet fishing isn't productive until the waters clear, usually in mid-July and best in fall.

Exceptions are large rivers, particularly below lakes, that usually manage to keep clear. Exam-

ples are the South Thompson River, just below Little Shuswap Lake, or the main Thompson, below Kamloops Lake. They are good in early July at times, bringing trout feeding activity every time the river levels start to drop, and continue productive right to late fall.

Since 90 per cent of British Columbia is above 3,000 feet elevation and lined with mountain ranges, the "classical" pastoral type stream is seldom found. Hence there isn't so much of that kind of stream fishing as tourist publicity may lead the angler to believe. Much more richly endowed are the northwest United States, particularly the still undammed tributaries of the Columbia River, the fine streams of coastal Oregon and northern California, and the headwaters streams of the Mississippi, rising in Idaho and Montana.

WHEN TO FISH

Best fishing hours on lakes are late afternoon and evening, in general, but rises or feeding spells can occur at any hour. Bait fishermen do well at daybreak but other lake fishing seldom is so outstanding in the small hours. Dry fly fishermen in particular get more action at the end of the day, and that usually includes the wet-fly fishermen. The latter take trout just under the surface, provoked into action by any hatch of flies. Sometimes shallow-water activity results at dusk in midsummer because only then does the surface water cool enough for the trout to bear it. It is shallow-water activity that makes for good trout fishing, particularly on the cast or trolled fly, but usually on any troll.

Various "activity" tables, such as the famous Solunar tables of the late John Alden Knight are intriguing to many anglers. Some swear by them - scientists do not. Back in the late 1940's, my newspaper, the Vancouver Sun, was offered the tables as the continent-wide syndicated feature it still is. My managing editor, when I asked about

using them, asked in turn "Are they reliable?"

I wrote to government fishery departments and some universities then noted for fishery work. Not one would agree that there is any scientific support for the tables, based as they are on the rhythms of the sun and moon. One did report what we already know, that commercial fishermen play the tides (as do many sport fishermen, with salmon). I couldn't find a reason for publishing the Solunar Tables as a regular service. So we never have to this day. Some newspapers and magazines do, however.

LIKELY FISHING SPOTS

Most of the trout activity in lakes is in the top 40 feet of water. That's where the oxygen is usually sufficiently concentrated to support marine life. Little light penetrates below 40 feet, so, since marine life depends upon photosynthesis -- the process of growth generated by light -- there is little plant or animal life beyond that 40-foot depth. Hence, the troller is advised to troll fairly shallow in lakes, unlike the sea-angler, who has water much more highly oxygenated, and to greater depths, as a result of tidal action.

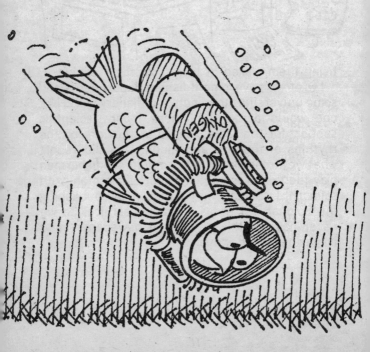

Most lake trolls and single lures are worked through the top 10 feet of water. Very deep, wire-line trolling rarely probes beyond 50 feet. If it does, it is a waste of time except, occasionally, with char in very large lakes. Char are better suited to low temperatures and minimal food supplies -- slow-growing as they are.

For most small-lake-trolling, the likely places are shallows off points and creekmouths. Sometimes trout move onto reedy flats in bays or lake inlets and outlets, where the flycaster and spinfisher often find their best action. The troller can fish there, too, but must take care not to snag into the reeds or into the lines of anchored, casting anglers.

Creekmouths are particularly promising. The creeks carry food and the fish know that, hanging off the creekmouth drop-offs and waiting for lunch to arrive. Such locales also are pleasant places to fish and easy to relocate.

In rivers, tributary creekmouths again are

hotspots, but the trout still prefer certain lies in the main river, in the proximity of those creeks. In small rivers, the fish lies are obvious enough -- in any dark streak where you can't see bottom and where a fish can hide from aerial predators. In all streams they try to take up position in the edge of the full flow, where they can hold without too much effort, yet observe food particles being swept past.

The swiftest water is at the surface in the middle of the stream, the slowest at the edges or shallows, and among the rocks or other rough spots on the riverbed. The angler must appreciate this so he can also appreciate how his bait or lure appears to a fish. If the bait is suspended from a float that is racing down the strong center-flow, the bait of course must also race along. But it likely is down in slower water and the final effect is that it is being drawn downstream at an unnatural speed, one reason baits and lures lift toward the surface when dragged downstream as fast as the surface water.

You must put yourself in the place of the trout and realize how silly a swiftly travelling bait appears in a parade of chips, pebbles or small, inert marine life, drifting along the bottom at a more leisurely pace. That's why you must have a weight associated with your bait or float-fished lure, to snag and generally retard the speed of the bait or lure.

If you are free-spinning or bumper-lead fishing, you cast across stream and sweep the river in arcs, from head of pool to tail. The hot-spots are the deeps and swirls among boulders, the edges of dark water, the heads and tails of pools. Seldom so productive are white water, large back-eddies and almost still, very deep pools.

OTHER USEFUL TACKLE

The landing net is, thinking positively, the next most important item to the rod-reel-line-lure in angling. Too often, the angler buys a tiny, short-handled item with chintzy netting that soon rots and lets a fish, usually the trophy-size, drop through it, to be lost.

Trout landing nets should be roomy, long-handled and of synthetic mesh. Cotton, whether or not oiled, eventually rots. If one must make a landing net do double duty on small streams and large lakes, then, sure, get one with a short-handle (or grip) used by stream fishermen but with the roomy basket hoop, no less than 12 by 18 inches, preferred for lakes.

In using the net, always scoop the fish from the head end, leading it across the net while the net is held, quietly, just under the water, then lifting sharply and surely as the angler lets the line and leader go limp. Experts also can scoop a trout, gathering the loose net bag in the forward hand and dropping it as the hoop is thrust sharply under the fish and lifted high, but don't try it the first time you hook a trout.

For river fishing, except in slow, pastoral streams, a net can be as cumbersome as helpful. Most river anglers play their fish to exhaustion, then slip them carefully ashore up a low part of the bank, or gingerly hoist them ashore. If expecting larger trout, steelhead, say, one should carry a light, sharp, jacknifing gaff-hook.

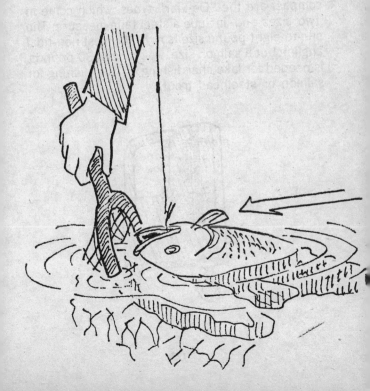

"HOW BIG WAS IT?"

A spring fish scale is handy. Most practical and compact are the "De-Liar" types, which come in two sizes and include a steel tape measure. The one-to-eight-pound size is right for most non-tidal angling but a salmon size, weighing to 30 pounds, is needed for lake char fishing or river fishing for salmon or steelhead trout.

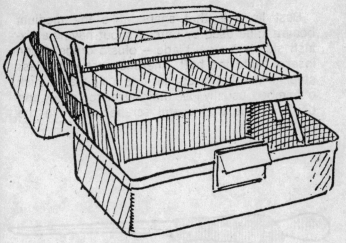

THE TACKLE BOX

Tackle boxes are really a must for lake fishing or for still-fishing on rivers where one stays put. Metal boxes have been outmoded by the many high-impact plastic boxes available. The latter don't corrode.

The old wicker creel doubles as a tackle box for some anglers who bought it, thinking it to be the traditional item. It's useful only for the river angler who wishes to stay in the water, dropping each fish into the creel as it is caught.

More useful for the river angler is the wrap-around steelhead "vest," a modified bird game carrier. The fly fisherman has a good selection of multi-pocketed waistcoats available. The latter are practical, except for carrying fish. But then, the classic fly fisherman doesn't figure on keeping (or even catching?) many trout, does he....?

Best knife is that shaped like the medium boning knife used by butchers, but having a six-inch stainless steel blade -- plus a crude spoon inserted into the butt. The cheapest - stainless steel knives that disappear into a simulated stick of bamboo, usually lose their edges too easily and don't include that useful scraper-spoon in the handle.

Extra supplies to be added to the lakefishing tackle box are insect repellant, suntan lotion, lip salve, headache tablets and a few band-aids, in addition to the small first-aid kit one should always carry. Be careful to keep insect repellant away from rod varnish and paint finishes. It seems to be an efficient paint remover.

And while it may sound sacrilegious in a land of calling loons, grebes and ducks, and chipping blackbirds, I often slip a tiny portable radio into my tackle box. One usually is near a town where periodic news casts -- or a bit o' rock -- help while away those hours between bites, no matter how mellow the atmosphere. Of course the radio isn't much use when using a motor, but I seldom troll, using the motor only to nip from hole to hole or back to the bivouac.

One should always take a fish container. Some optimistic friends of mine even take a large ice box aboard when fishing some of our productive inland waters in hot weather - cheeky fellows! Most of us carry a large plastic dishpan that will slip under a boat seat, and keep it covered with a water-soaked sack or old towel. The evaporating water lowers the temperature of the fish in the basin by several degrees.

FOOTGEAR

Waders are a must for river trouting and, since chest-high waders now can be bought for $10 up, they are easily the first consideration, rather than hip-waders. That is unless you never need to wade more than knee-deep, or unless there are long walks required to reach the fishing, and the weather is hot. Chest waders are steam baths in summer but delightfully cozy in cold or windy going.

I like boot-foot waders with felt or carpet soles glued on with weather-strip cement, trimmed to fit. Felt kits aren't cheap, $5 to.$10, but are great insurance against spills in slimy streams, and most are! Scrap carpet of synthetic material is much cheaper! Entire slip-on felt sandals also cost as much as the boots but are excellent and can be removed for long walks.

SLIP-ON TYPE FELTS

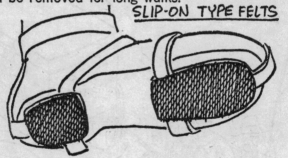

For purely lake fishing, a calf-high rubber boot is handy for lakeshore clambering in and out of the boat, and is much quieter when the angler is shifting about the boat itself, particularly in the ubiquitous aluminum boat. Some anglers slip off their boots, just to reduce vibration of sound through the boat hull and into the water.

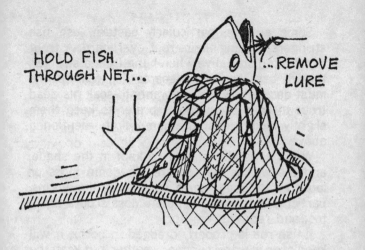

HOLD FISH.
THROUGH NET...

...REMOVE
LURE

"RELEASERS" AND "KEEPERS"

When liberating trout, one should be gentle. Wetting the hands guards against peeling off too many of the scales, which are an important protection against fungus and other external parasites. But wet, slippery hands make it more difficult to grasp the trout, hence one might crush its intestines or crack some ribs if intending to give it its freedom. I try to strike a balance, not deliberately drenching my hands but gently gripping the fish through the very adhesive mesh of the landing net, using long-nose pliers from my tackle box or fishing vest to remove the hook.

If I wish to keep the fish, I give it a smart crack across the skull, just back of the eyes, with those same pliers, a stick, the back of a jack-knife, or anything else handy. One friend of mine, a jolly chap, uses his bailing tin. A loud clang from the distance alerts us to the fact that he's caught another "keeper."

Some anglers, particularly eastern, use fish stringers, trailing their trout overboard. A trout won't often stay alive when hung from a stringer, though bass and other coarse fish will. So one must decide how long he wants to soak his dead trout to keep them cool. I prefer to keep them slightly moist under the damp cloth, mentioned above.

Worm cans also should be kept in the shade, and the worms well covered in damp moss or loose earth. Soggy earth soon sours the worms, particularly in warm weather. Moss scours them, too, and reddens 'em up.

If fish roe is properly dredged in borax, it will keep even in warm summer weather, but keep the container in the shade.

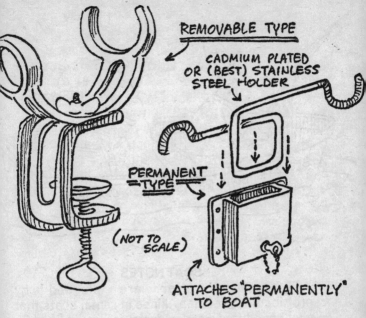

REMOVABLE TYPE

CADMIUM PLATED
OR (BEST) STAINLESS
STEEL HOLDER

PERMANENT
TYPE

(NOT TO SCALE)

ATTACHES "PERMANENTLY"
TO BOAT

ROD HOLDERS

Rod holders, more commonly seen in sea angling, are a much overlooked item for lake trolling. Many a lake marina doesn't even supply them, depending upon sticks jammed between inside and outside gunwales in wooden rowboats; otherwise into the oarlock sockets. There is an acceptable, cheap, thumb-screw rod holder of galvanized steel that mounts on an oarlock chock or gunwhale, and which is dismountable for stowing. It is a bit light and difficult to hold in place for heavy sea-trolling but serves for lake fishing if one uses rental boats.

If you have your own boat, then a good sea-rod-holder, with permanent base and detachable cradle, is a must, one on each side of the boat, even on the cartop boat and, yes, the canoe.

SLEAZY'S BOAT RENTS & USED CAR SALES   #73417

BOAT NOTES

Flyfishermen often are plagued by protuberances of many kinds in rental boats that may have fuzzy wooden surfaces, protruding bits of wire or nail, or just cracks here and there in the wood. It's a good idea to carry a four-by-six-foot piece of heavy canvas to lay in the bottom of such hairy craft (or in your own, if I've also described yours). That's for flaking out the coils of line as they're stripped in between casts.

If you like to row, pay attention to the condition of the oars and locks on rental boats. On your own boat, make sure the locks fit the chocks snugly. If you've a three-seater boat, add extra oarlock chocks at the front seat. It's handy with two anglers in the boat, the owner rowing from up front, well separated from his partner in the stern. With three passengers it of course doesn't matter if the oarsman is always confined to the middle seat.

Easily the most useful and popular boats are the beamy, 10-foot fiberglass and plastic, or the 100-pound-plus, 12-foot aluminum. If one fishes alone, he might like a shorter, lighter boat of well under 100 pounds, but will miss the leg room, not to mention the room for laying out spare rods.

Outboard motor horsepower needn't be great. Speeding anglers aggravate others. If one must make his ski boat serve for lakefishing, he should be as circumspect as possible about roaring from hole to hole. I like a six-horse, gearshift outboard for general use but most boats mentioned above are rated for 7½ to 10 horse motors. Aluminum boats that are whanged across the lake at top speed tend to loosen their rivets and leak. (Bullet holes from other disgruntled anglers could also be a problem!) They will stay watertight indefinitely if moved about at a gentle planing speed of, say 12 to 15 miles per hour.

One should always carry a spare propellor, shear pin (if the motor has a shear pin), set of plugs, plug socket wrench, pliers and motor manual. I like a five-gallon tank, though some fishing motors come with smaller tanks. The larger tank is cumbersome in the boat but never have I needed more than the five gallons for an entire weekend of fishing. I'd carry a spare if I trolled more, however.

CONCLUSION

In closing this book, the author probably isn't the first to feel he has just **started** to put across his message to other would-be trout anglers. I say "other" because all of us, no matter how long we've angled, no matter how long in our own bailiwicks, really never cease to be "would-be" Waltonians. There are so many new places, new methods, new sizes of fish and new tests that "would be"exciting to try.

I hope the reader of this book, if his search for angling knowledge has carried him this far, will have as much pleasure in his peregrinations as have I -- not just in catching fish; we soon manage that; but in catching the sights and sounds, the triumphs and the good companionship of angling.

Keep your hooks sharp and your camera cocked, and remember that angling is a sport and not a contest with other anglers.

More great reading designed to ensure your fishing success

All these books are available at your bookstore or sporting goods store — or you can order them directly from BC OUTDOORS on the convenient order form at the end of this book!

HOW TO CATCH SALMON — ADVANCED TECHNIQUES
by CHARLES WHITE & GUEST AUTHORS
The most comprehensive salmon fishing book available! Over 250 pages, crammed full of how-to-tips and easy-to-follow diagrams! Covers all popular salmon fishing methods: Downrigger Techniques, Mooching Trolling with bait; Tricks with Spoons and Plugs, Tips for river mouth fishing; Catching giant Tyees; Winter Fishing; Secrets of Dodger and Flasher fishing; Buzz bombs, Deadly Dicks, Sneaks and other casting lures – AND MUCH MORE!

$5.95

HOW TO CATCH SALMON — BASIC FUNDAMENTALS
by CHARLES WHITE
The most popular salmon book ever written! Contains basic information on trolling patterns, rigging tackle, fisheries Dept information on most productive lures proper depths to fish, salmon habit patterns how to play and net your fish, downriggers where to find fish! This is the basic book on salmon fishing in the North Pacific and now has been expanded and updated to include the Great Lakes region as well.

$4.95

HOW TO CATCH SHELLFISH!
by CHARLES WHITE

How, when and where to find and catch many forms of tasty shellfish! Oysters, Clams, Shrimp, mussels, limpets. Easiest way to shuck oysters. Best equipment for clamming and shrimping! When not to eat certain shellfish! What to eat and what to discard! Easy ways to open and clean shellfish! How to outrace a razor clam. A delightful book chock-full of useful information! Illustrated. **Newly Expanded Edition!**

$2.95

HOW TO CATCH CRABS!
by CAP'N CRABWELLE

Now in a seventh printing, with revisions that show latest crabbing techniques! Tells how to catch crabs with traps, scoops, rings! Where, when and how to set traps! Best baits! Detailed description and illustrations of a much easier method of cleaning, cooking and shelling the meat! A great book, crammed-full of all you need to know about **How to Catch Crabs. Newly Expanded Edition!**

$3.50

WHERE TO FIND SALMON —
Vancouver Island
by ALEC MERRIMAN

Where to Find Salmon combines catch dates and locations of more than 75,000 salmon caught in the season-long "King Fisherman" contest, as well as on-the-spot research, first-hand reports, and "local knowledge". Plus — Detailed maps of the "hot spots", and easy-to-read charts! Know when (and where) the runs arrive in each area, and plan your fishing trips accordingly! Fishermen using the information in this book are finding that the big runs of Salmon are showing up right "on schedule" each year! **New Expanded Edition $4.95**

DRIFTFISHING
by JIM GILBERT and others

Seven expert, Pacific Coast fishermen reveal experiences, secrets and instructions to help you become more productive using Perkin, Buzz-Bomb, Stingsilda, Deadly Dick, and herring.

Whether you fish salmon, bottomfish, trout, or other predatory fish anywhere in the world, this book of illustrated techniques for mooching, casting and jigging can help novice or expert increase their catch.

$5.95

HOW TO CATCH BOTTOMFISH!
by CHARLES WHITE

While salmon are the "Glamor" fish, bottomfish are everyday good eating — and easy to catch! This book shows how to catch Cod, Sole, Perch, Snapper, Rockfish, and other tasty bottomfish. Tells best tackle and rigs; baits; when and where to fish! Covers Drift-fishing, Trolling, Casting from shore. Plus easy-to-make "Super Lure"! Detailed step-by-step filleting diagrams! **Revised and Expanded.**

$2.95

HOW TO COOK YOUR CATCH
by JEAN CHALLENGER

A great companion for our "How-to-Catch" books! Tells how to cook on board a boat, at a cabin or campsite! Shortcuts in preparing seafood for cooking! Cleaning and filleting! Recipes and methods for preparing delicious meals using simple camp utensils! Special section on exotic seafoods! Illustrated

$2.95

BC OUTDOORS
FISHING GUIDE

to Fresh Water
in British Columbia

This is British Columbia's most comprehensive annual fishing guide. The directory covers all the province's fresh water fishing areas and is absolutely indispensable. You'll find special features by well-known fishing experts that will help you catch your limit and enjoy your sport to the full. An added feature is your own personal notes and log section, so you can keep a permanent record of your fishing successes and failures — vital information to help you plan future success. Don't miss the annual Fresh Water Fishing Guide, it's packed with information that you can't afford to be without.

$4.95

BC OUTDOORS
SALT WATER

Fishing Guide
to British Columbia

B.C.'s only province-wide salt water fishing guide has an easy-to-follow area directory to give you detailed descriptions of what you can expect to find in more than 225 fishing spots. Plus there are lots of special features by the experts to help you get the most from your fishing. The Salt Water Fishing Guide is illustrated throughout and you'll find a personal log section so you can record your successes for future reference.

$4.95

LOGGING ROAD TRAVEL

with ALEC & TAFFY MERRIMAN

Over TWO THOUSAND MILES of private logging roads on Vancouver Island are now open to the general public! AND CAN USUALLY BE EXPLORED IN THE FAMILY CAR OR CAMPER! Mile-by-mile guides through this backwoods wonderland! Exact mileages with detailed maps and directions. A vital part of any logging road outing!

Vol. 2 has kilometer equivalents.

Vol. 1—Victoria to Campbell River $5.95
Vol. 2—Campbell River
**   to Cape Scott $3.95**

PRINCE GEORGE BACKROADS

by KEN & KATHY BERNSOHN

It's still possible to have a lake all to yourself, to canoe, fish, or sit by the fire at dusk and listen to loons laughing.

There are still roads where you want to drive slowly and look at cathedral-like birches or giant firs   where you discover quiet campgrounds, salmon and trout, raspberries and roses

You'll find all of the mile by mile details described and mapped in this book.

$4.95

OUTDOORS
WITH ALEC MERRIMAN!

Features new Outdoors Fun Calendar telling how, when and where to enjoy the outdoors on Vancouver Island! Contains valuable data, expert tips on trout lies and steelhead runs. Stream by stream and pool by pool directions for best fishing spots. Expanded edition; new maps and illustrations; new fishing and hunting information!

$3.95

BOOK ORDER FORM

To: BC OUTDOORS BOOKS
202-1132 Hamilton Street,
Vancouver, B.C. V6B 2S2

Please send me the following books:

HOW TO CATCH SALMON
— Advanced Techniques _____ at $5.95 _____

HOW TO CATCH SALMON
— Basic Fundamentals _____ at $4.95 _____

HOW TO CATCH STEELHEAD _____ at $2.95 _____

HOW TO CATCH TROUT _____ at $3.95 _____

BUCKTAILS AND HOOCHIES _____ at $2.95 _____

HOW TO CATCH SHELLFISH _____ at $2.95 _____

HOW TO CATCH CRABS _____ at $3.50 _____

WHERE TO FIND SALMON _____ at $4.95 _____

DRIFTFISHING _____ at $5.95 _____

HOW TO CATCH BOTTOMFISH _____ at $2.95 _____

HOW TO COOK YOUR CATCH _____ at $2.95 _____

BC OUTDOORS FISHING GUIDE
TO FRESH WATER _____ at $4.95 _____

BC OUTDOORS SALT WATER
FISHING GUIDE _____ at $4.95 _____

A CUTTHROAT COLLECTION _____ at $5.95 _____

DISCOVER BARKERVILE _____ at $6.95 _____

LOGGING ROAD TRAVEL — Volume 1
— Victoria to Campbell River _____ at $5.95 _____

PRINCE GEORGE BACKROADS _____ at $4.95 _____

OUTDOORS WITH ALEC MERRIMAN _____ at $3.95 _____

EXPLORING BRITISH COLUMBIA
WATERWAYS _____ at $4.95 _____

TOTAL PAGE 1 $_____

TOTAL PAGE 1   _____

OKANAGAN BACKROADS — Volume 1
  — South Central Okanagan   _____ at $3.95 _____

LOWER MAINLAND BACKROADS

Volume 1 — Garibaldi to Lillooet   _____ at $4.95 _____

Volume 2 — Fraser Valley   _____ at $4.95 _____

Volume 3 — Hope to Clinton   _____ at $4.95 _____

Volume 4 — Garibaldi Region   _____ at $4.95 _____

      Sub total $_____

      Plus postage and handling**   _____

      TOTAL $_____

☐ My cheque for $_____ is enclosed
☐ Visa   ☐ MasterCard

_____
CREDIT CARD NUMBER   EXPIRY DATE

_____
SIGNATURE

_____
NAME

_____
ADDRESS

_____
CITY   PROVINCE   POSTAL CODE

    **Postage and handling charges:
      1 - 4 books — 50¢ per book
      5 or more — 35¢ per book

SPECIAL PRODUCT INFORMATION
FOR OUR READERS

We get many letters asking for our recommendations on purchasing fishing tackle, crab and shrimp traps, boating gear and other products related to the subject matter of our books.

To fill this need and to help those who cannot buy specialized equipment in their area, Charlie White Productions operates a mail-order division.

You can obtain a FREE catalogue, which includes the best tackle, traps and special items, such as an electric hook sharpener, automatic smokehouse, trap marker buoys, depth sounders and more, by writing to BC OUTDOORS, 202-1132 Hamilton Street, Vancouver, B.C. V6B 2S2.